What's So Great About Silent E?

The Thoughts of Sunnie Rae

Written by Deanna T. Thompson
Illustrated by Sunnie R. Thompson

AuthorHouse™
1663 Liberty Drive
Bloomington, IN 47403
www.authorhouse.com
Phone: 1-800-839-8640

First published by AuthorHouse   6/2/2010

ISBN: 978-1-4490-9274-0 (sc)

Printed in the United States of America
Bloomington, Indiana

This book is printed on acid-free paper.

authorHOUSE®

"What's so great about the letter E?" I asked myself one day. Sure, it's the first letter of big things like elephants and big emotions like exasperated.

But what about when a word ends with E? Most of the time, it makes no sound at all, so who needs it?

But then I

started thinking ...

With silent E,

I can ride a

TUBE

down a long, snowy hill.

Without silent E, I'd have to ride in a
TUB, which sounds fun too,
until you hit a bump, fly out of the tub,
and it lands on your head.
That would hurt, BAD!

I guess I'd rather
keep the silent E
so that I can ride
in a tube instead of
a tub.

Without silent E,

I wouldn't be

CUTE ...

I'd

be

CUT!

Like that time when I cut myself right on the end of my pointer finger, and every time I colored, or practiced writing my letters, it would hurt all over again.

Yes, I would definitely rather be

cute than cut.

Give me that silent E!

Without silent E,
my sister, Sarah,
wouldn't play the

FLUTE ...

She'd play the

FLUT!

What in the world is a flut?

Whatever it is, I bet it doesn't sound as pretty as a flute!

With silent E,

Superman can wear a

CAPE.

Without silent E, he'd have to wear a

CAP,

and that just doesn't seem right!

I bet he couldn't even fly without a cape.
What would be so super about him then?

Without silent E,
Grandpa wouldn't be able to use a

CANE ...

He'd have to use a
CAN! Oh no!

That sounds dangerous! He could fall down
and hurt himself, and that would be sad.

I love Grandpa very much, so please make
sure he uses a silent E.

With silent E, I can find

Australia on my

GLOBE

with no problem at all.

Without silent E, my globe would look like a big GLOB of continents and oceans all mixed together!

I may never find Australia!

Without silent E,

PINE

trees would be ...

PIN trees,

and the dear little birdies

might get poked!

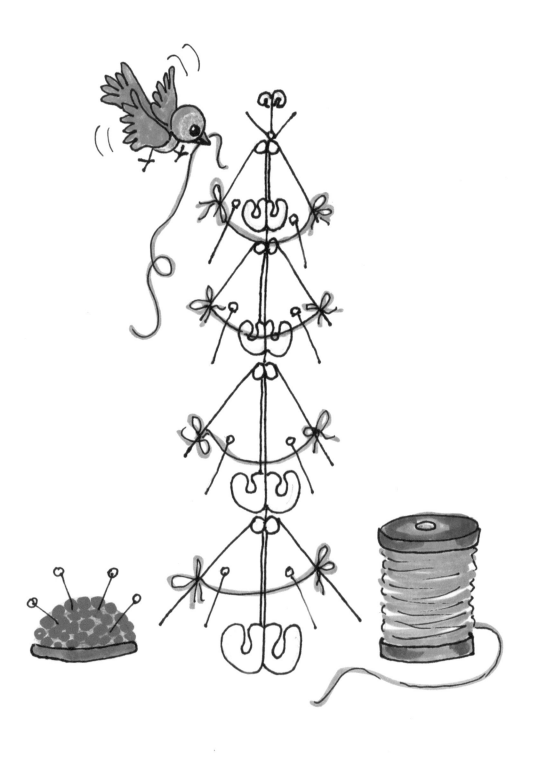

Without silent E, my little brother
PETE would be my PET.

(Hey, now that's not a bad idea!)

But do you know what else
would happen?

My
TAPE
would
TAP,

HOPE

would

HOP,

fruit

would   ,

my

ROBE

would

ROB,

(oh boy, that would really be bad!)

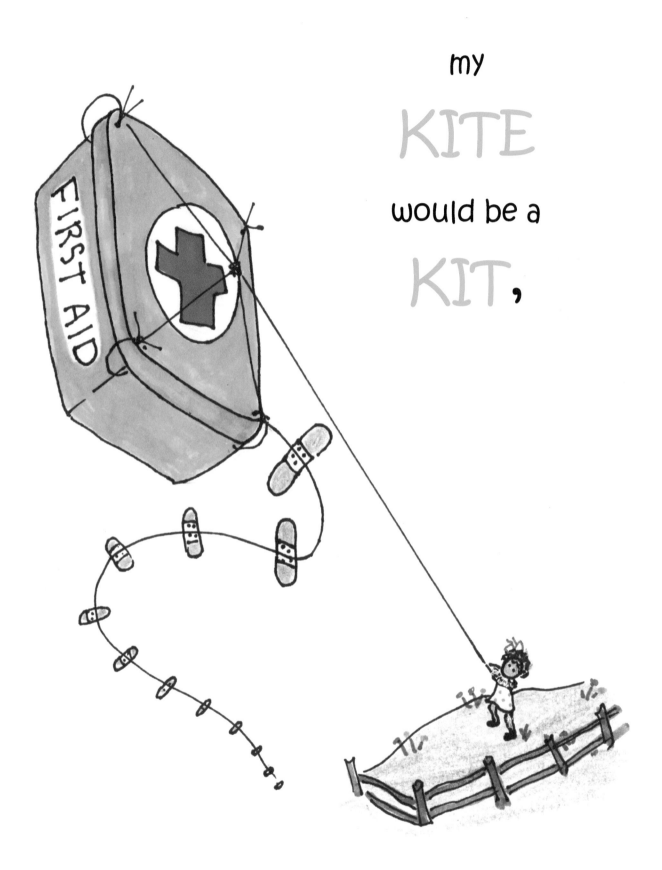

my

KITE

would be a

KIT,

and my

SPINE

would

SPIN!

WOW!

I believe I was

WRONG!

Silent E is VERY important!
What would we ever do without it?!

Thank goodness for

Silent E!

CPSIA information can be obtained
at www.ICGtesting.com
Printed in the USA
BVHW020312131119
563654BV00003B/14/P